T0076343

# MAN FROM NEBRASKA

⊰A PLAY⊱

## TRACY LETTS

NORTHWESTERN UNIVERSITY PRESS

EVANSTON, ILLINOIS

Northwestern University Press
www.nupress.northwestern.edu

Copyright © 2006 by Tracy Letts. Pub-
lished 2006 by Northwestern University
Press. All rights reserved.

Professionals and amateurs are hereby
warned that this material, being fully pro-
tected under the Copyright Laws of the
United States of America and all other
countries of the copyright union, is subject
to a royalty. All rights, including, but not
limited to, professional, amateur, record-
ing, motion picture, recitation, lecturing,
public reading, radio and television broad-
casting, and the rights of translation into
foreign language, are strictly reserved. All
inquiries regarding performance rights for
this play should be addressed to Ronald
Gwiazda at Rosenstone/Wender, 38 East
Twenty-ninth Street, Tenth Floor, New
York, NY 10016.

Printed in the United States of America

10 9 8 7 6 5 4 3 2

ISBN-10: 0-8101-2347-9
ISBN-13: 978-0-8101-2347-2

LIBRARY OF CONGRESS
CATALOGING-IN-PUBLICATION DATA

Letts, Tracy, 1965–
    Man from Nebraska : a play / Tracy
Letts.
        p. cm.
    ISBN 0-8101-2347-9 (pbk. : alk.
paper)
    I. Title.
PS3612.E887M36 2006
812.6—dc22
                            2006022310

♾ The paper used in this publication meets
the minimum requirements of the American National Standard for Information Sci-
ences—Permanence of Paper for Printed
Library Materials, ANSI Z39.48-1992.

*To the memory of my friend Katrin Cartlidge*

Canst thou by searching find out God?
Job 11:7

# CONTENTS

# PRODUCTION HISTORY

*Man from Nebraska* received its world premiere at Steppenwolf Theatre Company (Martha Lavey, artistic director; David Hawkanson, executive director) in Chicago, Illinois, opening on November 20, 2003. It was directed by Anna D. Shapiro, with set design by Todd Rosenthal; costume design by Mara Blumenfeld; lighting design by Ann Wrightson; original music by Shawn Letts; and sound design by Rob Milburn. Malcolm Ewen was the stage manager, and the production dramaturg was Edward Sobel. The cast was as follows:

| | |
|---|---|
| Ken Carpenter | Rick Snyder |
| Nancy Carpenter | Rondi Reed |
| Cammie Carpenter | Barbara Ann Grimes |
| Ashley Kohl | Beth Lacke |
| Reverend Todd | Thomas White |
| Pat Monday | Shannon Cochran |
| Tamyra | Karen Aldridge |
| Bud Todd | Richard Bull |
| Harry Brown | Michael Shannon |

MAN FROM NEBRASKA

## CHARACTERS

Ken Carpenter, *fifty-seven years old*

Nancy Carpenter, *fifty-four years old*

Reverend Todd, *forty-four years old*

Cammie Carpenter, *eighty-one years old*

Ashley Kohl, *thirty-one years old*

Pat Monday, *forty-nine years old*

Tamyra, *twenty-nine years old*

Harry Brown, *thirty-three years old*

Bud Todd, *seventy-five years old*

## PLACE

The outskirts of Lincoln, Nebraska, and London, England

## TIME

The present

## NOTES

Silences, comfortable and otherwise, should be allowed to speak as loudly as the text. The first few scenes in particular should take a great deal longer to perform than to read.

Both syllables of "lawzee" are given equal emphasis.

Dashes indicate an interruption; ellipses indicate an incomplete thought or a trailing off.

# ACT ONE

## FIRST MOVEMENT

### SCENE 1

[*Sound: suburban street sounds, hum of a car engine. A luxury sedan.* KEN *drives.* NANCY, *his wife, looks out the window.* KEN *drives. They sit in the car.* KEN *drives.*]

NANCY: They're finally going to tear down that ugly house.

KEN: Mm.

[*They sit in the car.* KEN *drives. Sound: church bells.*]

### SCENE 2

[*Sound: choir and parishioners singing a hymn. A Baptist church.* KEN *and* NANCY *stand.* NANCY *holds an open hymnal, but they know the song.*]

KEN and NANCY [*singing*]: "All on the altar, dear Jesus,
　　Master, I hear thy call.
　　Somehow I know thou canst use me,
　　I must surrender my all.
　　My all for thee,
　　My all for thee,
　　To give my all to thee, dear Lord.
　　Savior divine,
　　Henceforth is mine,
　　To live for thee,
　　Dear savior, for thee . . ."

[*The song ends. They listen to a sermon from* REVEREND TODD.]

REVEREND TODD [*from offstage*]: Thank you, good people. And thank
　　you, Imogene, for filling in beautifully on the organ for Mr. Spears,
　　who is visiting his grandson Kyle out there in California. We hope
　　Mr. Spears returns to us safely, of course, although someone told
　　me he's now playing the organ for some hippie heavy metal band.

[*Laughter.*]

　　We'll keep a good thought.
　　　　You know, this morning I'd like to take a look at the third part
　　of our relationship to God. Remember, over the last couple of
　　weeks, we talked about the first part, conversion, and the second
　　part, baptism, but now we want to consider part three, Christian
　　growth, and I'm going to tell you a story here that I hope illus-
　　trates our efforts to grow as Christians.


SCENE 3


[*Sound: Muzak rendition of "A Whole New World (Aladdin's Theme)."
Furr's Cafeteria.* KEN *and* NANCY *scan the restaurant, looking for a table.*

*They hold plastic trays laden with Salisbury steaks, mashed potatoes, creamed corn, coleslaw, lime Jell-O, light bread, iced tea. NANCY nods to a table. They unload their food from the trays. NANCY sits as KEN takes the trays offstage, then rejoins her. They pray, briefly, silently. They eat. They eat in silence. They eat.]*

NANCY: How's your steak?

KEN: Good. How's yours?

NANCY: Mm.

*[They eat in silence. KEN smiles, waves at an unseen acquaintance.]*

KEN: Hi, Don.

*[KEN and NANCY eat. They eat in silence.]*

SCENE 4

*[Sound: television, oxygen inhaler. A private room in a nursing home. CAMMIE breathes into an oxygen mask, sits in a wheelchair, pointed toward a TV show, an inane celebrity newsmagazine. The volume is quite loud. CAMMIE sits. She sits. She breathes. KEN and NANCY arrive in her room. KEN carries a Styrofoam food container. They pitch their voices louder when they speak to CAMMIE.]*

KEN: Hi, Mom.

NANCY: Well hello there, sleepyhead.

*[They take turns kissing her cheek. She offers little response. NANCY turns down the TV and removes CAMMIE's oxygen mask.]*

KEN: How are you feeling?

NANCY: You doing okay?

KEN: You look good.

NANCY: You sure do.

CAMMIE:: I'm hungry.

NANCY: We brought you some food.

CAMMIE: Oh, good. What'd you bring me?

[KEN *opens the container.*]

NANCY: What do we have—

KEN: We have some ham.

CAMMIE: Oh, good.

KEN: We have some peas.

CAMMIE: Gimme some ham.

KEN: We have some Jell-O.

CAMMIE: Gimme some ham.

[NANCY *feeds her, cutting the ham into tiny pieces with a plastic knife and fork.*]

NANCY: Natalie called last night.

[*No response.*]

KEN: Mom?

CAMMIE: What.

KEN: Nancy said—

NANCY: Natalie called last night.

CAMMIE: Who?

NANCY: Natalie. Your granddaughter.

CAMMIE: How's she doing?

KEN: She's doing real good, Mom.

NANCY: She said be sure and tell you hello, and she misses you, and she'll see you at Christmas.

CAMMIE: She working for Kenny?

KEN: No, that's Ashley who works with me. Natalie's in school.

CAMMIE: In school.

KEN: Yes—

CAMMIE: She's still in school?

KEN: She's getting her master's.

CAMMIE: Oh.

KEN: She's very smart, Mom. She's getting her master's at Brown.

CAMMIE: I don't know what that is.

NANCY: Where'd you get those pretty flowers?

CAMMIE: What?

NANCY: Where'd you get those pretty flowers?

CAMMIE: I don't know.

NANCY: You don't know.

[KEN *checks the card.*]

KEN: They're from Zora. That was sweet.

CAMMIE: Gimme some ham.

NANCY: You've got an appetite.

CAMMIE: I know it.

NANCY: Is it good?

CAMMIE: So good.

NANCY: So good, huh.

CAMMIE: Yes.

NANCY: Good, I'm glad.

CAMMIE: John was here.

[KEN *and* NANCY *share a look.*]

KEN: Was he?

CAMMIE: Yes.

KEN: Dad came by?

CAMMIE: Yes.

KEN: When did he come by?

CAMMIE: Last night. The middle of the night.

KEN: How's he doing?

CAMMIE: Fine.

KEN: What did he say?

[*No response.*]

Mom?

CAMMIE: Yes?

KEN: What did he say?

CAMMIE: What?

KEN: Dad, when he came by.

CAMMIE: Not much.

KEN: Was he glad to see you?

[CAMMIE *coughs, breathless, dry.* NANCY *fills a plastic cup with water, holds the cup while* CAMMIE *drinks, then replaces the oxygen mask over* CAMMIE'*s face.*]

Mom, was Dad glad to see you?

CAMMIE: Gimme some ham.

## SCENE 5

[*Sound: television. The living room.* KEN *and* NANCY *watch TV:* JAG, *say.* NANCY *scrapes at her nails with an emery board. They sit and watch television. They sit. They watch television. A phone rings offstage.* NANCY *exits. She can be heard talking to a friend.* KEN *sits and watches* JAG.]

## SCENE 6

[*The bedroom.* NANCY, *in a nightgown, sits on the edge of the bed, rubbing her hands with lotion.* KEN *enters, wearing pajama bottoms and a white T-shirt.*]

NANCY: Did you lock up?

KEN: Yes.

[*He kneels by the bed, prays silently.*]

Amen.

[*They get in bed.*]

Did you set the alarm?

NANCY: Yes, I did.

KEN: Good night.

NANCY: Good night, honey.

[*They kiss.* KEN *turns out the light. They settle.*]

## SCENE 7

[*The bathroom. The medicine cabinet fluorescent blinks on.* KEN *stands before the bathroom mirror. His T-shirt is soggy with sweat. He shakes insuppressibly, weeps, sobs. He grips the rim of the sink, grits his teeth, attempts to regulate his breathing. Can't. Collapses to one knee, runs cold water, splashes his face.* NANCY *approaches in the dark.* KEN *struggles to collect himself.*]

NANCY: Ken . . . ?

KEN: Go back to bed, honey.

NANCY: Are you all right?

KEN: Yes, I'm fine.

NANCY: Are you sure?

[*She approaches the doorway. He closes the door, talks to her through it.*]

KEN: I'm sure. Go back to bed.

NANCY: You don't sound good.

KEN: Please . . .

NANCY: Are you sick?

[*Silence.*]

Ken?

[*He opens his mouth to speak.*]

Open the door. You're scaring me.

[*He doesn't move.*]

I'm scared.

[*He doesn't move.*]

I'm coming in.

[*He raises his hand as if to bar the door but stops short.* NANCY *enters.*]

What's the matter? You look awful. Listen to me: Are you having a heart attack?

[*He shakes his head.*]

A stroke? Are you sick, honey? Talk to me.

[*He can't answer. He weeps. She approaches him with comforting arms. He spasms, retreats.*]

KEN: No. Stay away.

NANCY: All right.

KEN: Please. Don't crowd me.

NANCY: I won't.

KEN: Don't crowd me.

NANCY: I'm not.

[*They keep their positions. They keep their positions.*]

Breathe.

KEN: Right.

NANCY: Are you in pain?

[*He can't answer.*]

Are you in *physical* pain?

[*He shakes his head.*]

Breathe. Did you have a nightmare?

KEN: Kind of. No.

[*They hold their positions.*]

NANCY: Tell me what to do.

KEN: I don't believe in God.

NANCY: Okay. I don't understand.

KEN: I don't believe in God.

NANCY: What does that mean?

KEN: I don't think . . . there's a God. I don't believe in him anymore.

NANCY: What do you believe in?

KEN: I don't know.

[*They hold their positions.*]

NANCY: What do you *think* you—?

KEN: Maybe we're just . . . *science*. Like they say. Accidental science.

NANCY: All right—

KEN: That doesn't matter. I don't know what I believe in. It doesn't matter. But I don't think there's a man in heaven, a God in heaven. I don't believe there is a heaven. We die and . . . we're done, no more, just . . .

NANCY: All right . . .

KEN: Nobody listens when I pray. We're not rewarded for what we do right—

NANCY: —Ken—

KEN: —punished for what we do wrong—

NANCY: All right.

KEN: Nancy. I don't understand the stars.

NANCY: What does that mean?

KEN: The stars. In the sky. Don't make sense. To me. I don't understand them.

[*Silence.*]

NANCY: Did something happen? To make you feel this way?

KEN: I don't know—

NANCY: To make you change—

KEN: I don't know, I just . . .

NANCY: Have you done something wrong?

KEN: No. No. I mean, *yes.* No, I just realized, I had a . . .

NANCY: A nightmare—

KEN: No—

NANCY: A *vision*—

KEN: No, NO! A, a, a, a *flash* . . . *flashes,* for days now, a . . . *clear moment.* I don't know, my head is clear! I can't talk about this, Nancy, I don't know what it means—

NANCY: All right—

KEN: I can't, I don't have . . . these aren't . . . *thoughts.* This isn't a *decision.*

NANCY: Okay. I understand.

[*Silence.*]

Tell me what to do.

KEN: Go back to bed.

NANCY: I don't want to leave you like this.

KEN: Please.

NANCY: Please, honey—

KEN: Please go back to bed—

NANCY: Please don't make me go to bed. I don't want to go to bed. How can I go to bed?

[*Silence.*]

Can I get you something?

KEN: No.

NANCY: Something for your stomach? Some milk?

KEN: No.

NANCY: I'll put on some tea for us—

KEN: Don't handle this. Stop handling me, please. I don't have a stomachache, or a headache—

NANCY: All right.

KEN: I'm not sick.

NANCY: Just talk, talk to me.

[*Silence.*]

Ken?

KEN: I have nothing to say to you right now, honey.

NANCY: Ken—

KEN: What can you do?

NANCY: I—

KEN: I don't understand the stars. Is there anything you can do about that?

NANCY: How can I do anything about that? I don't know how—

KEN: Can you explain the stars?

NANCY: No.

KEN: Then you can't do anything. There's nothing you can do.

## SECOND MOVEMENT

### SCENE 8

[*The kitchen.* NANCY *serves breakfast to* KEN.]

KEN: Better.

NANCY: Yes?

[KEN *nods.*]

Do you think you need to . . . you should talk to someone?

KEN: You mean a doctor.

NANCY: Maybe.

KEN: No. I don't know.

NANCY: Reverend Todd.

KEN: I don't know.

[*They sit in silence. They sit.*]

I think . . . maybe I should just sit with this for a while.

NANCY: So you still feel the same way.

KEN: Yes.

NANCY: I don't understand.

[*Beat.*]

I can't pretend to understand. How can something that was there yesterday not be there today?

KEN: I don't know. Are you asking me?

NANCY: I asked you.

KEN: I don't know.

NANCY: You don't know much, do you?

KEN: No.

[*Silence.*]

I'm sorry.

NANCY: Don't apologize.

KEN: I don't know what's happening.

NANCY: Help me understand.

KEN: How can I do that?

NANCY: Did you believe in God yesterday, at church?

KEN: I suppose so.

NANCY: At lunch, at the grocery store, in the *garage*? When did you stop believing? *Did* you have a dream?

KEN: I didn't have a dream. It's a feeling. I can't tell you when I first felt it.

NANCY: Sounds like an empty feeling.

KEN: Yes.

NANCY: A bad feeling.

KEN: I don't know. Maybe.

NANCY: Well, isn't empty bad?

KEN: Not necessarily.

NANCY: Explain that to me.

KEN: I can't.

NANCY: All right.

KEN: Empty isn't bad if it's the truth. The truth can't be bad, can it?

NANCY: I disagree.

KEN: I guess it depends on who you are—

[NANCY *flings her glass of juice across the room.*]

NANCY: That was the truth. Wasn't that bad?

KEN: No. I don't think so.

NANCY: Are you going to work?

KEN: Yes, of course.

NANCY: As if that's obvious.

KEN: No, I just mean . . . yes, I'm going to work.

NANCY: Are you planning on telling your daughter this piece of news?

KEN: Why is she suddenly *my* daughter?

NANCY: Are you?

KEN: I hadn't thought about it.

NANCY: I'm just frustrated.

KEN: It's okay.

NANCY: I'm not mad at you . . .

KEN: It's okay if you are.

NANCY: Maybe I am.

KEN: Let me just . . . let me just be with this.

NANCY: Maybe it'll pass.

KEN: Or maybe I'll . . . Maybe it'll pass, right.

NANCY: Or maybe you'll what? What?

KEN: No, just maybe I'll have to figure something else out.

NANCY: What does that mean?

KEN: If it doesn't *pass,* I'll have to figure something else out.

NANCY: Something else.

KEN: Some other way.

NANCY: Why?

KEN: Because there would have to be another way.

NANCY: A better way.

KEN: Another way, yes, a better way. An *only* way.

NANCY: Don't get mad at me.

KEN: I'm not.

NANCY: I'm trying to understand.

KEN: Me too.

[*Silence.*]

NANCY: A better way.

## SCENE 9

[*The office.* KEN *sits across from* ASHLEY *at her desk. She eats a bag of food from McDonald's.*]

ASHLEY: . . . I told Renata to get me an estimate on that Land Cruiser, the Lewises' Land Cruiser, and I'd process the rest of it for her. And she goes, "I did." I go, "Where's the form?" She goes, "There's a form on that?" I go, "Renata, you been here a month, how many of these you filled out now? Course there's a form." She goes, "I only—

KEN: Ashley. I'm sorry. I have a problem.

ASHLEY: What.

KEN: Uh. I've had a crisis.

ASHLEY: What's the matter?

KEN: It's hard to explain. It's nothing like what you're thinking.

ASHLEY: Okay. What.

KEN: I've had a crisis. Of faith.

[*Silence.*]

ASHLEY: Does Mom have cancer?

KEN: What? No.

ASHLEY: Is Mom sick?

KEN: She's fine. No, no, it's—

ASHLEY: Oh my goodness.

KEN: No, it's nothing *like* that.

ASHLEY: My goodness, you really scared me.

KEN: Sorry—

ASHLEY: I thought you were going to tell me Mom had cancer, and then I thought—

KEN: No, I'm sorry—

ASHLEY: Thank goodness. All right now, a crisis of faith. You've had a crisis of faith.

KEN: Yes, of faith. In God.

ASHLEY: In God.

KEN: Yes.

ASHLEY: *Why?* When did this start?

KEN: I'm not sure exactly.

ASHLEY: Uh-huh—

KEN: But it seems to me as if it's tied up with . . . with everything.

ASHLEY: Everything.

KEN: My life, *way* of life, um . . . routines. My routine with your mother.

ASHLEY: With Mom.

KEN: And the job, and the, the . . . town.

ASHLEY: Lincoln.

KEN: Yes.

ASHLEY: Your crisis of faith is . . . I don't understand. It's related to Lincoln?

KEN: I guess . . . I just . . . I don't . . . Do you ever look around? At the people around you, their habits and their, their . . . things they do. The way they live, that we live. Do you ever think about the . . . the food we eat and think about where the food comes from, where it goes? All the people. I'm not being clear.

ASHLEY: I'm, I'm—

KEN: Or the way . . . people swing their arms. When they walk. Downtown, at lunchtime, and all these people walk in and out of buildings and swing their arms. They don't think about it, there's no decision, they all just *swing their arms.*

ASHLEY: It has something to do with balance, right? Or—

KEN: Where does your faith come from?

ASHLEY: My faith.

KEN: Your faith in God, the church, the Baptist faith . . . God. Forget the rest, where does your faith in God come from?

ASHLEY: It's divine.

KEN: No, come on.

ASHLEY: It . . . I got taught by *you.* I got it from you and Mom.

KEN: Right, from me. You got it from me. And your mother.

ASHLEY: And then other people and stuff—

KEN: Your pastor—

ASHLEY: —yeah, and Sunday school and teachers—

KEN: Right, but if it hadn't been for me—

ASHLEY: And the Bible, I read the Bible—

KEN: If I hadn't believed, taught you to believe, taken you to church, you wouldn't have that.

ASHLEY: I guess.

KEN: That's what I'm . . . That's blind. Not blind, but it's, that's not, it's not . . . it isn't, that isn't *made.* You didn't *make* that. You didn't—

ASHLEY: Make what?

KEN: You didn't *earn* your faith.

ASHLEY: How are you supposed to earn it?

KEN: I don't know, experiences.

ASHLEY: What experiences? I've had experiences. I've been outside of Lincoln.

KEN: I know.

ASHLEY: I've been to Washington, D.C. And Philadelphia—

KEN: Right—

ASHLEY: I've been to Florida. I've been, I went to Holland with the Chorettes.

KEN: Ashley. I know. I'm sorry. I'm not making sense. I don't know what I mean.

ASHLEY: I think you should talk to Reverend Todd.

KEN: You're right.

ASHLEY: Or just a friend, you know? Someone you can relate to.

KEN: Did you know, I was thinking about this: I don't have any friends.

ASHLEY: Oh, please—

KEN: No, no, I'm not . . . I just, that's funny, I had the same thought: I should talk to a friend. And then I tried to think of one, but I couldn't. I don't have any.

ASHLEY: I'm your friend.

KEN: Of course you are, sweetheart, I was—

ASHLEY: Natalie's your friend, why don't you call Natalie?

KEN: No, I, you know, she's busy at school—

ASHLEY: I don't exactly know what you're talking about—

KEN: No—

ASHLEY: —but I know how it feels to look around and wonder if things would be different if you'd done things different, you know?

KEN: You do?

ASHLEY: Sure. Everyone does.

KEN: And what would you do different?

ASHLEY: Well . . . nothing.

KEN: So what do you think about? Are you talking about Greg, your job—?

ASHLEY: Like, remember when me and Greg looked at that plot out in Eagle Grove?

KEN: Eagle Grove.

ASHLEY: That subdivision out past the country club—?

KEN: Right, right—

ASHLEY: We talked about building the colonial style. With the duck pond?

KEN: No, right.

ASHLEY: I wonder if that was a bad move, passing on that. 'Cause when they built out that spur on 34, that land just went *whoosh*, you know? I mean, it's not like we don't like our place; we love it, you know, and the kids, that's their home, but still.

*[She puts her arm around him.]*

When's the last time you had a checkup? Are you feeling okay?

KEN: Yeah, I'm fine.

ASHLEY: What does Mom say about all this?

KEN: She. She said what you said: Talk to Reverend Todd. She says she doesn't understand.

ASHLEY: You two aren't fighting, are you?

KEN: No.

ASHLEY: Okay. You okay?

KEN: I'm ashamed.


## SCENE 10

*[The kitchen.* NANCY *and* REVEREND TODD *sit, drinking coffee.]*

REVEREND TODD: We have a great speaker this Wednesday night: Mark Tidwell. He's a character.

NANCY: I'm afraid we don't get out to church on Wednesdays anymore.

REVEREND TODD: Hm.

NANCY: Not like we used to.

REVEREND TODD: He uses puppets.

NANCY: Oh.

REVEREND TODD: I know how that sounds. I know that sounds queer. But he's real good. The puppets are actually very artistic. Not just kiddie stuff. But the kids especially like him.

NANCY: I'm sure they do.

[*Silence.*]

REVEREND TODD: Dad wanted me to be sure and say hello. To both you and Ken.

NANCY: Oh, well, you say hello to him for us, would you?

REVEREND TODD: You've met Dad, right? Have you met Dad?

NANCY: Yeah, uh-huh.

REVEREND TODD: We have dinner every Friday at Applebee's.

NANCY: That's nice. I hope you didn't . . . did you tell him about Ken's troubles?

REVEREND TODD: No, I just said I was coming over for a chat—

NANCY: Good. Oh, good—

REVEREND TODD: Though Dad would get it. He's certainly had his struggles with faith.

NANCY: Really? You understand, it's just that I'm not comfortable with—

REVEREND TODD: He was in the war, World War II, and some of his experiences really . . . I mean, hey, these stories.

NANCY: I'm sure.

REVEREND TODD: Ken was in the military, wasn't he?

NANCY: He was in the Air Force. But not during wartime. He was between wars.

REVEREND TODD: Dad was a POW.

NANCY: I didn't know that.

REVEREND TODD: In the European theater of operations.

NANCY: Dear.

REVEREND TODD: He ate a man. In the POW camp. Germans retreated, packed up, headed for the hills, but they left the prisoners locked up. Before the Allies liberated the camp, Dad's cell mate expired from starvation. So Dad had to eat him to keep from starving himself.

NANCY: That's awful.

REVEREND TODD: Yes.

NANCY: Oh. That's awful.

REVEREND TODD: Yep. Oh, yeah.

NANCY: Can I get you some more coffee?

REVEREND TODD: No, ma'am, I'll be up all night.

NANCY: I think I still have some coconut cake—

REVEREND TODD: Can you imagine that? Eating another human being?

NANCY: No, I sure can't.

[KEN *enters.* REVEREND TODD *stands.*]

KEN: Hello.

REVEREND TODD: Hidy, Ken.

[*They shake hands.*]

KEN: Hi, sweetheart.

NANCY: Are you mad at me?

KEN: No. A little on the spot.

REVEREND TODD: Sure.

NANCY: I've just . . . I haven't known what to do with myself for a *week* now—

KEN: Nancy. It's okay. You did good.

NANCY: Can I pour you a cup of coffee?

KEN: No, thanks.

[*The three of them look at one another.*]

NANCY: There's cake.

[*Silence.* NANCY *exits.*]

REVEREND TODD: How you been?

KEN: Okay.

REVEREND TODD: You play any golf lately?

KEN: Not much. I went out a couple of weeks ago.

REVEREND TODD: We've had the weather for it.

KEN: Yes. You?

REVEREND TODD: Nah. I hit some balls last weekend, but.

KEN: Mm.

REVEREND TODD: Somebody tells me you carry a four handicap.

KEN: Noo.

REVEREND TODD: What's your handicap?

KEN: Nine.

REVEREND TODD: Still. You know what I can't get used to? I worked
with a pro this past spring and he kept trying to break me of the
habit of looking at the ball.

KEN: Oh, right.

REVEREND TODD: You know what I mean, on your drive.

KEN: Right.

REVEREND TODD: 'Cause, you know, all your life, you hear, "Keep your eye on the ball." But when you *drive*—

KEN: Right.

REVEREND TODD: Well, *you* know. Nine. Jeez.

[*Silence.*]

How you like the team this year?

KEN: We'll see. Tough schedule.

REVEREND TODD: Ain't it a bitch. Just the conference alone. You know what I think it is? Ever since Devaney left—

KEN: What, what did Nancy tell you?

REVEREND TODD: She says you may be . . . maybe you're confused.

KEN: Maybe.

REVEREND TODD: You want to talk about it?

KEN: Mm.

[*Long silence.*]

REVEREND TODD [*sotto voce*]: Ken. Is this something you can discuss . . . in your home?

KEN: Sure. Where else would I talk about it?

REVEREND TODD [*sotto voce*]: I just thought . . . maybe Nancy doesn't need to know *everything.*

KEN: No. Nothing like that, no, this is . . . this doesn't have anything to do with—

REVEREND TODD: Okay.

KEN: No, I . . . some questions have come up for me . . . I thought I had answered, or maybe never asked. But it's started me thinking . . . a lot of areas . . . a lot of decisions I've made . . . my choices are maybe based on the wrong set of . . .

[*Another long silence.*]

REVEREND TODD: "Seek and ye shall find," buddy.

[*Silence.*]

Know what I mean?

KEN: No.

REVEREND TODD: "Ask and ye shall receive." "Seek and ye shall find." "Nothing worth having ever comes easy." Right?

KEN: Uh-huh. It's just that . . . I grew up in the church.

REVEREND TODD: Right—

KEN: I've had God and the Baptist faith in my life since I was . . . since I can remember.

REVEREND TODD: Praise the Lord. When were you saved?

KEN: Twelve?

REVEREND TODD: Sure.

KEN: And I think maybe I've just never considered it. I've always just accepted—

REVEREND TODD: But now you have doubts.

KEN: That's an understatement.

REVEREND TODD: Everything else checks out? Your marriage is sound?

KEN: Yes.

REVEREND TODD: Kids are healthy?

KEN: Yes.

REVEREND TODD: Grandkids healthy?

KEN: Yes.

REVEREND TODD: You're healthy?

KEN: Yes.

REVEREND TODD: How about your mom? I know she has to wear on
   your mind—

KEN: Well, that's—

REVEREND TODD: I know that's tough—

KEN: That's, that is what it is, I can't—

REVEREND TODD: What can you do, right—

KEN: —ask Nancy to—

REVEREND TODD: —no, of course—

KEN: —I mean, Mom's past any semblance of—

REVEREND TODD: —sure, I know, *I know.*

KEN: So, no, I don't know, I don't know where this—

REVEREND TODD: You been feeling low?

KEN: I haven't been feeling anything.

REVEREND TODD: When's the last time you had a vacation?

KEN: You mean took time off work?

REVEREND TODD: Vacation. When's the last time you left Lincoln to do something fun?

KEN: We went to the OU game down in Norman—

REVEREND TODD: With the church group.

KEN: Yes.

REVEREND TODD: How about just you and Nancy?

KEN: I suppose . . . when Natalie graduated school. Iowa.

REVEREND TODD: Did you spend the night?

KEN: No. No, wait, we just had Nancy's family reunion in Wichita—

REVEREND TODD: When's the last time you took a trip *by yourself*?

KEN: Alone. Just me.

REVEREND TODD: Yes.

KEN: Convention. In Denver.

REVEREND TODD: Insurance convention.

KEN: Yes.

REVEREND TODD: When.

KEN: Twenty years ago.

REVEREND TODD: Ken. Get the heck out of Lincoln for a while. Take a couple of good books with you. What books do you like? You a mystery reader? History buff?

KEN: I like Westerns.

REVEREND TODD: Now you're talking, old son. Grab a toothbrush, pack some clean shirts, some Louis L'Amour paperbacks, and get yourself gone.

KEN: What about Nancy?

REVEREND TODD: I'll bet Nancy could use some time away from you, too.

KEN: Yeah . . .

REVEREND TODD: This is my job. Insurance is your job, faith is mine. Faith takes work. Sometimes you need a break.

KEN: Really.

REVEREND TODD: Look here, I got a little land up north, coupla hundred acres, and I go up and work on it every Saturday. You ever do that kind of work?

KEN: Yes.

REVEREND TODD: So you know what I'm talking about. I had an old boy help me get up this bodarc stump, musta been a hundred years old, roots the size of your thigh. We started on it at five A.M., Saturday morning. We were still sweating over that mother at three. A hundred degrees. If we'd kept working, we would've had it up by six o'clock, three more hours. Know what I did?

KEN: No, I—

REVEREND TODD: "Go home." We went home. We showed up next Saturday and had that stump out of the ground and loaded on the back of my truck in less than an hour. You got to build up your strength. Get tired? Have a rest. This race is long distance, not a sprint.

KEN: Right.

[*They stare at each other.*]

REVEREND TODD: Like the ad says: "Where was it you wanted to go, anyway?"

# THIRD MOVEMENT

## Scene 11

[*Sound: jet engine. An airplane.* KEN *sits in a first-class seat.* PAT *sits beside him.*]

PAT: First trip to England?

KEN: I beg your pardon?

PAT: Is this your first trip to England?

KEN: I was stationed . . . I was stationed there. In London.

PAT: In the Army.

KEN: Air Force. Almost forty years ago.

[*Silence.*]

PAT: Business trip or . . . ?

KEN: I'm sorry?

PAT: Business?

KEN: No . . . business, no. I . . .

PAT: Pleasure then.

KEN: Yes: pleasure.

PAT: Nothing wrong with pleasure.

KEN: No. I guess not.

PAT: I'm business.

KEN: Oh.

PAT: I split time between London and the States.

KEN: Really. Do you have a place in London?

PAT: Work provides me with a pied-à-terre.

KEN: That's nice.

PAT: Your wife couldn't make it?

KEN: Hm.

PAT: I noticed your ring.

KEN: No, I.

PAT: That's a shame.

[*Silence.*]

KEN: I wish she could've come. It's not that kind of trip.

PAT: Oh.

KEN: Yes.

PAT: So maybe not . . . *pure* pleasure then.

KEN: Maybe not.

PAT: Pat Monday, Coca-Cola.

KEN: Ken Carpenter.

PAT: Pleasure to meet you.

[*Silence.*]

   I'm divorced.

KEN: I'm sorry.

PAT: I'm not the first.

KEN: I suppose not.

PAT: I've gotten philosophical about it.

KEN: Good.

PAT: I think these things are always for the best. Even if it doesn't seem that way at first, or for a long time even. I don't think you get fired from a job unless you really didn't want the job to begin with.

KEN: Huh. So it was . . . mutual.

PAT: What's that?

KEN: Your divorce was—

PAT: No, actually, he divorced me. But that's what I'm saying. I thought the marriage was what I really wanted.

KEN: It wasn't.

PAT: As it turns out.

KEN: Good for you.

PAT: I get laid whenever I want.

KEN: Oh.

PAT: Not that that's what I'm talking about, but still. I just mean. I'm not hurting.

[*Silence.*]

   No, he asked for the divorce. He was cheating on me, and he asked for the divorce. Right?

KEN: He told you that, that he was cheating?

PAT: I *saw* him.

KEN: Saw him—

PAT: Saw him, in the act, with another woman.

KEN: In the act—

PAT: In the *act. Physically.*

KEN: Oh, my goodness—

PAT: I didn't say anything. He never knew I saw.

KEN: Why didn't you say anything?

PAT: I was embarrassed, I guess. Ahh. Seems silly.

KEN: I don't know.

PAT: No?

[*A long silence.*]

Where are you staying?

[KEN *takes a pamphlet from his coat pocket, hands it to* PAT.]

Leicester Square Sheraton. Nice. You'll like it, very centrally located, nice rooms.

KEN: Good.

PAT: Kind of small. Welcome to Europe. My place isn't far from yours, maybe I'll stop in some night and we can have a drink.

KEN: Yes. Sure.

PAT: Would you like that?

KEN: Sure.

PAT: To see me again. I think you would.

KEN: I'm sorry. You think I would what?

PAT: Like to see me again.

KEN: Well, sure.

PAT: Better not let me get away.

[*The plane hits a sudden jolt. Drinks tip over, lights blink.*]

OH MY GOD!

[*The plane steadies.* PAT *reaches in her bag for some pills.*]

I gotta take these pills if we're going to hit turbulence. May I have some of your . . .

[*He gives her his water. She takes the pills, downs them with the water.*]

I fly a hundred thousand miles a year, and I'll never get used to it.

[*She pulls a blanket around her shoulders.*]

KEN: I don't know if this helps you at all, but I don't think it matters.

PAT: What doesn't matter?

KEN: If the plane crashes.


## SCENE 12

[*Sound: light jazz. The cocktail lounge of the Leicester Square Sheraton.* KEN *sits alone, eats nuts from a glass bowl, drinks a ginger ale, plays with the foreign money on his tabletop. A black cocktail waitress,* TAMYRA, *sits at the bar, reading a paperback book.*]

KEN: Kind of slow, huh?

TAMYRA: Afternoons are like that here. Once summer's past.

KEN: I'm here. I'm staying here, in the hotel.

[*She smiles politely.*]

Are you from London?

TAMYRA: Mm-hm.

KEN: I'm from Nebraska.

TAMYRA: Oh.

[*Silence.*]

That's right in the middle, isn't it?

KEN: Yes.

[*Again, silence.* TAMYRA *returns to her book.*]

Can I ask what you're reading?

TAMYRA: Poetry.

KEN: Really.

TAMYRA: Mm-hm.

KEN: Who's the writer?

TAMYRA: You know a lot of poets?

KEN: No.

[*She considers, holds the cover of her book out for him to read. He takes reading glasses from his shirt pocket, puts them on, takes the book from* TAMYRA, *and holds it at arm's length.*]

"Pablo . . . NAIR-YOU-DAH."

TAMYRA: "Neruda."

KEN: "Neruda." Hm. You speak Spanish?

TAMYRA: A little. But this is translated.

[*He opens the book.*]

KEN: So it is.

[*He returns the book. She resumes reading. He takes off his glasses. Another long silence.*]

I've never known anyone who read poetry. Unless they had to.

TAMYRA: Why would you ever have to?

KEN: For school.

[*She resumes reading.*]

It never held much interest for me. Poetry. As a subject. As a kind of writing.

TAMYRA: As a form of literature.

KEN: Right.

TAMYRA: You prefer other forms.

KEN: I suppose so.

TAMYRA: You need a narrative.

KEN: Right.

TAMYRA: A story.

KEN: Yes.

TAMYRA: Otherwise, how would you ever get from here to there?

KEN: You must get a lot of reading done on the job.

TAMYRA: It's usually very quiet.

KEN: I understand.

[*Quiet.*]

Is your home not quiet?

TAMYRA: Not all the time. I have a flatmate.

[*She returns to her book. Feels him staring. She puts her book down, turns to him.*]

And what brings you to London?

KEN: Uh . . .

TAMYRA: Business?

[*He can't answer.*]

Hello?

KEN: Um.

TAMYRA: Don't worry yourself.

[*She returns to her book.*]

KEN: I don't believe in God.

TAMYRA: Join the club.

KEN: That's why I'm here. Because I stopped believing in God.

TAMYRA: Yanks toss you out for that now?

KEN: No, I left. I decided to leave. To clear my head, maybe . . . find some answers.

TAMYRA: Good luck. But if you came to England looking for God, you're going to be disappointed. He hasn't been seen round here since the Crusades.

KEN: I'm Ken.

TAMYRA: Tamyra.

KEN: Tamyra. That's pretty.

TAMYRA: Thank you.

KEN: I don't know why I'm here, really. My pastor recommended it.

TAMYRA: Your pastor recommended London. What, is he C of E? You have that in Nebraska, do you?

KEN: He recommended I take a trip. London was *my* choice.

TAMYRA: Why?

KEN: I was here. Many years ago.

TAMYRA: A bit of reminiscing then.

KEN: I suppose.

TAMYRA: Back in the day when you were *shaggin'* some *limey bird*?

KEN: What?

TAMYRA: Had a woman here, did you?

KEN: No . . .

TAMYRA: It's all right if you did. Good a reason as any to come to London. Better, actually.

KEN: That's not why I came. I'm married. London just seemed like the right distance. Foreign but . . . not too foreign.

TAMYRA: More foreign than you can imagine.

KEN: It doesn't look the same.

TAMYRA: I bet you don't either. You have kids?

KEN: Two daughters. Grown daughters.

TAMYRA: Nice.

KEN: Mm-hm.

TAMYRA: What.

KEN: Nothing.

[*Beat.*]

I'm thinking I didn't do a very good job with them.

TAMYRA: How's that?

KEN: I wish I had done things different.

TAMYRA: Like what?

KEN: I'm not sure. I think my parents did a better job of raising me than I did of raising my own kids.

TAMYRA: Did you tell your daughters you love them?

KEN: Yes.

TAMYRA: I think that's kind of tough to improve upon. Another ginger ale?

[KEN *shakes his head.*]

Would you like an alcoholic beverage?

KEN: I don't drink.

TAMYRA: Why not?

KEN: I just don't care for it.

TAMYRA: Maybe you haven't been drinking the right stuff.

KEN: What do you recommend?

TAMYRA [*considering*]: No. Someone else can corrupt you if they want. I don't need it on my conscience.

KEN: No, it's all right. I'm an adult.

TAMYRA: Grapefruit juice. Am I right? In the morning, you drink grapefruit juice.

KEN: Very good.

TAMYRA: A salty dog for you. Ken. Very salty.

KEN: I like the sound of that.

TAMYRA: Because my friend Ken doesn't like it too sweet. My friend Ken needs something a little savory. Or maybe even a little bitter.

KEN: Right . . .

TAMYRA: For his adventure. For his narrative.

# ACT TWO

## FOURTH MOVEMENT

### SCENE 1

[*Sound: light jazz. The cocktail lounge of the Leicester Square Sheraton.* KEN *and* TAMYRA. *Days later.* KEN's *had a few.*]

KEN: There used to be a good place round here to get fish-and-chips. Serve 'em in newspaper, rolled-up newspaper. Sauce . . . brown sauce . . . soaks the paper. You had to be careful your chips didn't mush outta the bottom of the paper onto your uniform. Catch it from the CO.

I didn't mind the Air Force . . . but I didn't like it. Sure, the rotten food, all that ketchup, I mean, the food, the hours, the . . . "maggot" this and "hillbilly" that and all the rest, lots worse, the cursing, but you know all that before you ever sign up. I don't like all those *men.* Everywhere you went there were all these *men* there. Men seem so dull after a while. And they're all the same, especially in the military, 'cause I guess they're supposed to be. I know that sounds like a joke, but it's true, really true: they are just the same. Some are a little more quiet, I guess, but lawzee if the only difference you can find between people is their *volume*. I just couldn't find a reason to spend time with those fellows. We had nothing to learn from each other.

One boy, a colored boy—a black boy, a young black man, from Oklahoma, named Eamonn Pitts . . . we got on pretty good 'cause we were from the same part of the country, I guess. He was a good ballplayer, too, good shortstop. We palled around some, took our chow together. Saw some of the city, too, saw London. Y'know, a guy like me, where I come from—I guess that's one of the good things about the military, 'cause a guy like me, where I come from and what I do, would never really have an opportunity to, to . . . uh, spend time with black people, hardly even see a black person, if it weren't for the Air Force. I had never really known black folks. The janitor at my high school, but even he . . . I think he might've been part Indian. And a girl, a little colored girl who propositioned me when I was a little boy, told me to meet her in this abandoned building after school and she'd . . . show me some things. I didn't go. I was young.

Eamonn, though . . . we were friends. He was quiet. We were quiet together. We didn't mind being quiet together.

TAMYRA: You're not still mates, are you?

KEN: No. No. We never spoke again after the service.

TAMYRA: What did you have to learn from him?

KEN: Hm?

TAMYRA: You said you had nothing to learn from the other fellows.

KEN: Oh. I don't know. Grace . . . ?

TAMYRA: Planning on seeing any of London this go-round?

KEN: I walked through Hyde Park this morning.

TAMYRA: Yeah?

KEN: Walk in the park.

[PAT *enters.*]

PAT: Well, there you are.

KEN: Hello. Pat.


## SCENE 2

[KEN *and* NANCY's *living room.* NANCY *and* ASHLEY.]

NANCY: We agreed we wouldn't call. We decided calling might defeat the purpose.

ASHLEY: Who is "we"? You decided that?

NANCY: I agreed to it. What else can I do?

ASHLEY: You talk like agreeing to his terms is your only option.

NANCY: Isn't it?

ASHLEY: No, you could've said, "Walk out that door and I'll divorce you so fast your head will spin"—

NANCY: Marriage doesn't work like that—

ASHLEY: *My* marriage works like that. "I don't believe in God so, hey, I'm off to London." If Greg ever pulled a stunt like that with me—

NANCY: What if he did?

ASHLEY: Then we'd be through, end of story—

NANCY: It gets complicated when you get older—

ASHLEY: What were those vows about then? Why'd I stand up there in front of all those people and a preacher and all the rest of it and make "solemn vows"?

NANCY: Let's think about that then, shall we? Didn't you vow to stay together through sickness and health?

ASHLEY: Yeah, "stay together"—!

NANCY: Your father is sick right now, and we're going to get through this—

ASHLEY: Why are you defending him—?

NANCY: I'm sure it would make you happy if I drew a line in the sand and vowed to divorce your father if he crossed it—

ASHLEY: Make me *happy*—?!

NANCY: —but I'm not built like that. I'm going to stay with my husband, even when times are tough, if that's all right with you.

ASHLEY: But will Daddy stay with you?

NANCY: Your father is taking a vacation. He's entitled to that.

ASHLEY: What are you entitled to?

NANCY: Maybe I'll take a vacation when he gets back. All right? Now can we drop it?

ASHLEY: I called Natalie.

NANCY: Please don't tell me you bothered your sister with this.

ASHLEY: I thought she might want to know Dad's left you!

NANCY: I am really put out with you.

ASHLEY: I asked her to come here and stay with you.

NANCY: She's missing school. To come here and do what? You know how hard her school is, how far behind she'd get—

ASHLEY: Don't worry, she's not coming.

[*Beat.*]

[*Off* NANCY's *reaction*] Yeah. She said this wasn't any of her business.

NANCY: She's right.

ASHLEY: She made some stupid speech about how we're all "free agents." She called us "free agents."

NANCY: I'm not sure what that means but—

| | |
|---|---|
| NANCY: —your sister marches to the beat of her own drummer— | ASHLEY: She meant she doesn't feel like she belongs to our family anymore— |

NANCY: That's not what she said—

ASHLEY: It means our family is falling apart.

NANCY: Ashley. Please. Please.

ASHLEY: All right.

[*Silence.*]

Do you want to come stay with us?

NANCY: No, thank you.

ASHLEY: Do you want me to stay with you?

NANCY: Honey, you have enough to look after.

ASHLEY: I'd feel better if someone was here with you.

NANCY: Why do I have to have someone here with me?

ASHLEY: Someone's always been here with you.

# SCENE 3

[*Sound: light jazz.* PAT's *darkened apartment.* KEN *and* PAT *are kissing. They kiss tentatively at first. Then* PAT's *kisses become hungrier. They kiss. They break.* PAT *holds* KEN's *hand, pulls him gently toward the bed.*]

KEN: Wow.

PAT: Yeah . . .

KEN: Wowee.

PAT: I like the way you taste.

KEN: I like the way you taste, too.

[*She goes for him. They kiss. She rubs against him and he backs away.*]

PAT: I want you, baby . . .

KEN: Wowee.

PAT: I want you to take me.

KEN: I don't know.

PAT: I want you to fuck me.

KEN: Yeah, I've had a lot to drink.

PAT: You salty dog.

[*She kisses him greedily. He starts to pull away, but she won't let him. She wrestles him to the bed, throws him down, looms over him.*]

KEN: I haven't been with another woman in a long time.

PAT: Other than your wife. Other than Laura.

KEN: Nancy.

PAT: Nancy.

[*She sticks her tongue in his mouth.*]

KEN: I haven't been with another woman in forty years.

PAT: That's probably why you're so excited.

KEN: Probably, but that wasn't my point.

PAT: I want you to do me like your whore—

KEN: I don't know—

PAT: —like your little whore—

KEN: I don't know if I can—

PAT: Sure you can. Just stick me . . .

KEN: Gosh, you have a really nice apartment . . .

[*She takes off her top.*]

Oh, lawzee—

PAT: C'mon, baby, stick me.

KEN: Lawzee, I can't do that.

PAT: What's stopping you, big boy?

[*She puts his hands on her breasts.*]

KEN: I can't stop thinking about my wife.

PAT: That gets me hot.

[*Kiss.*]

I need you to do something for me.

[*She gets off* KEN, *reaches under the bed, pulls out a set of black plasticine restraints.*]

KEN: What are those?

PAT: I need you to tie me down.

KEN: What? Why?

PAT: I need you to be the boss. I've been such a bad girl.

KEN: Listen, you don't understand: I don't think I can do any of this. I can't make love to you—

[*She wraps a leather strap around her breasts.*]

PAT: Show me I've been so bad. Pinch my nipples.

KEN: I don't want to.

PAT: Pinch my nipples, baby—

KEN: No!

[*She stares at him. Sheds the strap, grabs her blouse.*]

PAT: Well, what in God's name are you doing here?

KEN: I'm sorry, I'm not experienced.

PAT: Jesus, I know that. You don't have to be. I'll do it. I'll take care of everything. I'm the woman. Goddamn it. I'll take care of everything.

KEN: I'm, I'm confused about some things—

PAT: —that's all right—

KEN: My heart's not in this. This isn't what I need.

PAT: —whoa, whoa, shh—

KEN: I shouldn't have come here.

PAT: I can do this. Y'know? I'm . . .

KEN: I just had to get away, from, to rest my, my, to spend time with, with my—

PAT: Jesus Christ.

KEN: —with my thoughts. On the advice of my pastor.

PAT: On the advice of your pastor? [*Laughs.*] So now that I bring the cuffs out, you think maybe this isn't what your pastor had in mind?!

KEN: Pat. I like you. I think you're really . . . lovely and . . . strong. And honestly, I came here with every intention . . . I've had too much to drink, and I can't hold my liquor, and that's not an excuse, I . . . I don't think this is what I . . . I think this will only confuse me more.

PAT: You're scared.

KEN: Yes, I am.

PAT: You're scared.

KEN: Yes.

[*They stare at each other. She puts her hand behind his head, pulls him gently to her. She holds him in an embrace. They slowly rock. They caress each other . . . backs, arms, necks. They kiss.*]

I just . . . I can't . . .

[*They kiss.*]

## SCENE 4

[*Sound: television, oxygen inhaler.* CAMMIE'*s private room.* CAMMIE *sits in her wheelchair, pointed toward a TV game show:* Family Feud, *say. The volume is quite loud.* CAMMIE'*s oxygen is off. She sits. She sits. She breathes.* NANCY *sits beside her, transfixed by the television, a tray of half-eaten food in her lap. They sit. They watch television. They sit.* CAMMIE *coughs.* NANCY *gives her water, then places the oxygen mask over* CAMMIE'*s face.* CAMMIE *breathes.*]

## FIFTH MOVEMENT

### SCENE 5

[*Sound: light jazz. The cocktail lounge of the Leicester Square Sheraton.* TAMYRA, *coat on, prepares for the end of her shift: register and bar business.* KEN *broods over his drink.*]

KEN: I called my wife last night. First time since I've been here . . . three weeks. She didn't answer.

TAMYRA: Leave a message?

KEN: We don't have an answering machine.

TAMYRA: Seems a wee bit Mennonite.

KEN: I'm afraid of the telephone. Afraid it'll bring me bad news.

[*Beat.*]

Can I get another?

[*She prepares a drink.*]

I don't have anything to say anyway.

TAMYRA: You've had a lot to say to me.

KEN: You're easy. You're just the bartender.

[*Silence as she finishes making his drink and places it in front of him.*]

I don't really know why I called her.

TAMYRA: Maybe you miss her.

KEN: I don't really know what I'm doing here.

TAMYRA: Your spiritual adviser recommended you take a vacation. So you vacated.

KEN: It isn't working.

TAMYRA: Then go home.

KEN: Y'know, as long as I can remember . . . I could look at something and I knew how my wife *felt* about it. It's scary to suddenly have nothing in common with anyone.

TAMYRA: How are you different?

KEN: Not different, just . . . separate. In church, I look around . . . I have a secret world in my mind, and if they could see it, they might . . . I don't know. Stone me.

TAMYRA: Why, is it sexy?

KEN: Sometimes. What it really is . . . what it really is, is free.

TAMYRA: Free. You lack freedom, so you fantasize about it.

KEN: Mm.

TAMYRA: Free.

[*More bar business.*]

Why do you think I'm nice to you?

[KEN *stares at her.*]

Aside from pouring your drinks, wiping your table, because it is my job, I listen to your stories, ask you questions, lend a sympathetic ear. Why do you suppose that is? Have an opinion?

[*He stares.*]

For the money. I'm nice because you tip well. Europeans don't tip, you know. It's not part of our culture. Americans tip because Americans speak the language of money. That's your language, Ken. Money. You pay me to be nice to you. So I am.

KEN: Are you saying you don't like me?

TAMYRA: No. I like you. But I've grown weary of your shite. I have a life of my own, you know, outside of this stupid bar. With my very own problems and . . . inabilities.

KEN: Inabilities.

TAMYRA: The inability to make any money. The inability to get out of this asinine job. The inability to fall in love with a straight man. All of these require more energy and attention than I care to give to you. Pining for freedom when you have more of it than anyone in the history of this earth.

KEN: More than you.

TAMYRA: Fucking-A. You sit there on your lily-white American ass and talk to me about freedom? The secret world in your mind, separate from the other white-bread motherfuckers sitting around you in church? In Lincoln-fucking-Nebraska? You've got to be fucking kidding me.

KEN: I'm sure I didn't mean freedom in the way you mean it—

TAMYRA: I'm sure you didn't either, but let me assure you, freedom only comes in one cast.

KEN: Which is?

TAMYRA: You'd have to be denied it to know.

[TAMYRA *starts to exit.*]

KEN: Please don't walk out on me.

TAMYRA: I must say, you seem fine to me.

KEN: Just talk to me.

TAMYRA: Staying in a posh hotel, drinking salty dogs, getting laid—

KEN: I need help.

TAMYRA: Why don't you get your girlfriend to help you?

KEN: She's not my—please.

TAMYRA: Why should I? I'm just the bartender.

[*She exits.*]


SCENE 6

[*Sound: streets of London.* TAMYRA *stands in a wet, cold London doorway.* KEN *approaches her tentatively, stands beside her.*]

TAMYRA: You can't journey to London, then stay in the Leicester Square Sheraton, or even Leicester Square, for that matter. Leicester Square,

Covent Garden, the West End's designed for you lot, for Americans, to feel like America's gutless version of England. You'll get as authentic an experience at Epcot Center.

KEN: Why isn't Epcot authentic? [*Off her look*] I mean, isn't *everything* authentic?

TAMYRA: A nun's habit is authentic, but wearing one doesn't make you a nun.

KEN: I don't think my problem has to do with where I'm staying.

TAMYRA: Then you never really needed to leave Lincoln, did you, Dorothy? No more talking about you. Here's Harry.

[HARRY, *wet, puffing on a soggy cigarette, his hand bandaged, shuffles into the doorway, regards* KEN *askance.*]

HARRY: Who's this?

TAMYRA: Harry, Ken. Ken, this's my flatmate, Harry.

KEN: Ken Carpenter. Nice to meet you.

HARRY: Is he serious? I have loads of bad news and a spot of good news.

TAMYRA: Let's have the bad news.

HARRY: I busted the key in the lock of the front door to our building. Rather, the key crumbled in my hand as if it were made of gingerbread. I smashed the window to reach my hand through and open the door and, in the process, severed a tendon and had to go to hospital, where they sewed ten black stitches into my wanking hand. Upon my return to the flat, I discovered our landlord's haggard wifey weeping on the sidewalk in front of the building. I assured her I intend to pay the two months' back rent owed her husband, as well as a reimbursement for the smashed window, although I would appreciate if he would consider at least splitting the locksmith's fee for the busted key, as I felt it was not my fault the key was made of gingerbread. At that point, she confessed that her husband, Jim, our landlord, actually expired some thirteen weeks ago. I offered that this certainly shed some light on his noticeable absence from the building and his inattendance to our affairs, particularly the faint yet menacing odor of natural gas emanating from the stub of rusting pipe inexplicably jutting from the center of my bedroom floorboards, a situation I have been willing to overlook given our tardiness with the rent payment. She then told me that the reason we have been heretofore uninformed of his demise is purely at his request. According to her, he croaked these final words: "Don't tell anyone I'm dead." She has been reeling from this instruction, unsure of at least two things: just how many people he actually intended by the word "anyone" and for just *how long* she was expected to keep this secret to herself. Apparently, my time to be kept in the dark amounted to approximately thirteen weeks. I was disheartened to learn, however, that within that thirteen-week period, our good landlord's crippling and clandestine gambling addiction was posthumously discovered, and as a result, our new landlady has been made aware by her accountant that due to tremendous debts incurred by said husband, the need has arisen for her to raise all rents by a shocking sixteen percent, the maximum allowed by our rental agreement. Her accountant has also encouraged her, as accountants will do when given the opportunity, to collect all outstanding debts in short order, and that if overdue payments are not indemnified, to take steps to rectify the situation. This means, in short, dear Tamyra, that you and I are currently responsible for rent payments of six hundred and forty pounds. And in twelve days' time, we will owe, not including any overdue utility invoices that have mayhaps slipped their magnetic shackles and drifted ignominiously between the fridgie and Formica, a grand total of one thousand and ten pounds sterling.

TAMYRA: The good news is you won the sweepstakes.

HARRY: No, although I did stumble upon a half-eaten Kit Kat bar in the pocket of my raincoat and therefore know how a sweepstakes winner must feel.

TAMYRA: That's not the good news.

HARRY: No. The good news is I scored.

[*He pulls an aspirin bottle from his pocket and gives it to* TAMYRA. *She shakes out pills, swallows one, offers one to* HARRY, *who declines.*]

I'm already well on my way.

[*She gives one to* KEN.]

TAMYRA: Swallow this.

KEN: What is it?

TAMYRA: Just do it.

HARRY: Are you giving my drugs away to elderly Americans then?

KEN: I don't take drugs.

TAMYRA: Another shocking revelation.

KEN: No, thank you.

TAMYRA: Take it.

HARRY: He doesn't want it.

TAMYRA: Shut up. Take it.

HARRY: I don't even know who the fuck this bloke is.

TAMYRA: Ken.

KEN: Tamyra.

TAMYRA: Take it.

KEN: Tamyra—

TAMYRA: Take it! Take the pill! Take drugs! Take the pill and swallow it! Eat the pill! Swallow the pill! Take drugs, take drugs, take drugs—

[HARRY *joins in.*]

TAMYRA AND HARRY: —take drugs, take drugs, take drugs!

TAMYRA: TAKE IT!

[KEN *swallows the pill.*]

## SCENE 7

[*Sound: loud dance music. A dance club. Fluorescent lights, colored lights, flash, strike . . . strike the dance floor, bounce, move.* KEN, TAMYRA, *and* HARRY *dancing. Of course* KEN's *awkward, even comical. But he's into it, even allows himself to dance with* HARRY *some. And* TAMYRA *and* HARRY *aren't laughing . . . well, yes, sure, they're laughing, but they're not judging. They're just dancing. Tripping, dancing. Joy. They dance. They dance.*]

## SCENE 8

[TAMYRA *and* HARRY's *flat.* KEN, TAMYRA, *and* HARRY *enter, buzzing.* HARRY *brings in paper sacks of kebabs, chips, sauce, sodas, whiskey, messily serves all. A pale sheet covers a standing object, about the size of a human.*]

KEN [*re flat*]: Wow. This is really . . .

TAMYRA: Small.

HARRY: Small.

KEN: It is really small.

TAMYRA: London's expensive.

KEN: Even in this neighborhood?

HARRY: Even in the East End, darlin'. Ketchup, anyone? Ken? You look like you could use tomatoey paste.

KEN: Yes, please. [*Re kebab*] Man, that's good.

HARRY: Don't they have kebabs in Nevada?

KEN: Nebraska. No, they don't—

HARRY: Nevada, Nebraska.

KEN: There's a big difference.

HARRY: Yes, I'm sure the good people of Nebraska actually manage to eat more fried butter per capita or some—

TAMYRA [*putting on music*]: You tell him, Harry. Nevada, Nebraska: Oxford and Cambridge, right?

HARRY: You bitch.

KEN: I don't get it.

TAMYRA: Harry matriculated at Oxford. Oxford don't much care for Cambridge.

HARRY: Toffs.

TAMYRA: Oxonians don't talk like Harry. His lower-class accent is an affectation.

HARRY: "Working class," if you please—

TAMYRA: Yes, *working* class—

HARRY: —and "affectation" isn't fair—

TAMYRA: Right—

HARRY: "Homage" is more like it, to the *genuine* people of this shite country . . .

KEN: You don't like your country?

HARRY: I wouldn't say that, Kenneth dear. I would, in fact, say that I *abominate* this shithole, second only to the godforsaken, sunblasted, bullet-riddled abattoir known as the United Cunts of America—

TAMYRA: Whoa, whoa, whoa       KEN: Now wait just a second—
now—!

HARRY: No, please, I will not discuss politics with the man from Minnesota.

TAMYRA: Nebraska—!       KEN: Nebraska—!

HARRY: I know!

KEN: Can I respond to your comment?

HARRY: No! Tamyra, get me out of this!

TAMYRA: Don't look at me, you're the one who took off on—

KEN: That's right—

HARRY: Oh, God, look! Ken. Be reasonable—

KEN: Why can't we talk about this?

HARRY: Because I'm not going to change your mind, and you're not going to change mine.

KEN: Is that important? What if we agree?

HARRY: I doubt very seriously you'd embrace my scenarios for change. Quite a few of them conclude with the question of how best to display great numbers of severed heads on pikes.

KEN: That's okay—

HARRY: And although I'm sure I could learn much from your vast experience of eating massive amounts of gristle in America's heartland—

TAMYRA: That's not—

HARRY: —truth is, your defensiveness would make me uncomfortable. I don't care for defensiveness. Only expression interests me, and, to a lesser extent, definition. But defensiveness bores me because it all sounds the same.

KEN: Why would you think I'm defensive?

HARRY: All Americans are defensive. You can't help it. You've seen the Beginning of the End, and it scares the shit out of you.

TAMYRA: Now you're doing all the talking. Try listening for fuck's—

HARRY: You're right, I'm sorry. Ken, I didn't mean it. America is the best, and I jest love MacDonald's, and Britney Spears, and all them Bushes and the other shrubbery, and I jest plum wisht I had my twenny-two. All right?

KEN: All I want to say is that we're both lucky to live in countries where we can have a conversation like this.

HARRY: Well reasoned, old man, words of wisdom, truly, morally sound, ethically unimpeachable. You are a noble sage—

TAMYRA: Shut up.

HARRY [*to* TAMYRA *re* KEN]: It's what you reap when you swap culture and education for aggression and capitalism.

TAMYRA: *We've* got culture. What's our excuse?

HARRY: We don't have one.

KEN [*re sheet*]: What is that?

TAMYRA: That's Harry's work.

HARRY: *Under* the drapery, not the drapery itself.

KEN: Can I see?

HARRY: No, you may not.

TAMYRA: Let him see it.

HARRY: He can see it when it's finished.

TAMYRA: He won't be here when it's finished.

HARRY: Then he can't see it.

KEN: But what is it?

TAMYRA: Just show it to him.

HARRY: Under no circumstance.

TAMYRA: You're an asshole.

HARRY: Nevertheless.

TAMYRA: So, Ken, you were saying, we're lucky to live in open societies where we might have these kinds of conversations.

KEN: Well, if you consider the *alternatives.* Way I see it, the whole idea of America is that any person has the right not only to speak their mind—

[HARRY *can take no more. He leaps to his feet, takes the sheet in his hand.*]

HARRY: Ladies and gentlemen, I am honored to present a work *in process*. Because it is in process, please, I must insist: no critical review will be allowed, either immediately or later, in any form, be it spoken or written, sighed or sputtered. This especially includes *praise*. (Praise is a killer.) Without further ado, then, allow me to present *Untitled Study, No. 16*.

[HARRY *removes the sheet, revealing a stone sculpture of a nude woman, her hands raised skyward in a gesture of supplication. Only the top half of the sculpture is completed; the lower half is merely an immense block of stone. It is apparent* TAMYRA *is the model for this sculpture. The work is extraordinary. Silence.*

HARRY *returns to his kebab.* TAMYRA *studies* KEN, *trying to gauge his reaction. She finally returns to her drink.* KEN *bursts into tears.* TAMYRA *and* HARRY *stand motionless, studying* KEN.]


# SIXTH MOVEMENT

## SCENE 9

[KEN *and* NANCY's *kitchen.* NANCY *and* REVEREND TODD *hold hands across the tabletop. Their heads are bowed, their eyes closed.*]

REVEREND TODD: . . . and, Lord, we ask that you keep watch over these good people in their troubled time. We ask that you guide Ken through his terrible blinding storm to find his way safely back to you. And we ask that you help this patient Christian woman in her long hour of disquiet. We ask these things in your name, O Lord, assured of your infinite wisdom and in the bosom of your eternal love. Amen.

NANCY: Amen.

[NANCY *has been quietly crying.*]

Thank you. I broke down at the market today. The checkout girl asked what was bothering me and I told her I had a bladder infection. I didn't know what else to say.

REVEREND TODD: I think you have to get out of the house more often. Go shopping at the mall. Play some bingo out at the bingo parlor. Go see a movie—

NANCY: I don't have the concentration for anything like that. And I do get out; I manage to make it over to the nursing home most every other day.

REVEREND TODD: You're shouldering quite a burden for yourself.

NANCY: Oh, she's no burden. We'll all be in that wheelchair soon enough.

REVEREND TODD: I'm talking about trying to have some fun. I'm talking about meeting new people, or at least enjoying your own company. Promise me something. Just . . . look out for yourself a bit. Get Ashley to take you to a dumb movie. Go out to that new steak house they built not two miles from here. You know what I'm talkin' about, that Outback Steakhouse?

NANCY: Yes.

REVEREND TODD: I'll bet you haven't even set foot in that place.

NANCY: I cook a better steak than they can.

REVEREND TODD: And how's about this: Let's see you in church a little more often. Little miss. We got Wednesday night prayer meeting; Sunday school, you could teach a Sunday school class; revival this Monday: free pizza.

NANCY: I like pizza.

REVEREND TODD: Get involved, 'cause we're there for you.

NANCY: I know.

REVEREND TODD: You promise me?

[*Doorbell rings.* NANCY *rises.*]

NANCY: I don't know who that could be.

REVEREND TODD: That's my daddy.

NANCY: Here?

REVEREND TODD: Yes, ma'am, he's picking me up for supper.

NANCY: Here.

REVEREND TODD: I think he wanted to say hello to you, if that's all
    right.

[NANCY *looks at* REVEREND TODD. *The doorbell rings again. She goes
offstage. Open door, greetings, et cetera. She enters with* BUD.]

BUD: Say, this is a heck of a place, ain't it, Ginny?

NANCY: Thank you.

REVEREND TODD: Don't she keep a nice place?

BUD: Would you look at that? What is that, mahogany?

NANCY: I'm not sure.

BUD: I'd say it is. [*Whistles appreciatively.*]

REVEREND TODD: Dad's a bit of a wood nut.

NANCY: Is that right?

BUD: Since I was a little splinter. [*Winks at* NANCY.]

REVEREND TODD: He practically whittled his apartment out of a block
    of wood.

BUD: Now, Ginny, don't go braggin' on me just 'cause there's a pretty lady here.

NANCY: Did you say "Ginny"?

BUD: Did I? [*Winks at* NANCY.]

REVEREND TODD: Short for "Virginia." Where I was born.

BUD: Don't go tellin' lies to the pretty lady, Reverend. You weren't born nowhere near Virginia and you know it; you were born right over there in Omaha.

REVEREND TODD: All right.

NANCY: Then what's the name Virginia for?

BUD: Nan, it's where the boy first became a twinkle in my eye.

NANCY: Oh.

[BUD *winks at* NANCY.]

Mm.

REVEREND TODD: Are you ready to eat?

BUD: I'm afraid I've embarrassed the boy. These young folks get downright jumpy when the talk turns to [*whispers loudly*] S-E-X. [*Winks at* NANCY.]

REVEREND TODD: Should we eat?

BUD: Did I see an Outback Steakhouse over on, what is that, Locust?

REVEREND TODD: Yes, sir.

BUD: Why don't we give that a go? I think I already pinched all the bread over at that Applebee's.

REVEREND TODD: We could.

BUD: Or maybe all I pinched were buns. [*Winks at* NANCY.]

REVEREND TODD: We could go there, that's fine.

BUD: What kind of food you think they got over at that Outback?

REVEREND TODD: Steak.

BUD: "Duh. Steak at a steak house? Dude, that is so lame." Is it Australian? Is that why it's called Outback?

REVEREND TODD: I think it has an Australian theme, yes, sir.

BUD: But the food isn't Australian, is it?

REVEREND TODD: Are you asking me if it comes from Australia?

BUD: Do I look like a damn idiot? I know the goldarn food don't come from Australia. You think I'm asking if some dumb Australians put a bunch of raw steaks on a slow boat to send to Nebraska?

REVEREND TODD: What *are* you asking?

BUD: Is their food prepared in some kind of Australian fashion . . . ?

REVEREND TODD: I don't know.

BUD [*to* NANCY]: Let's find out, shall we?

NANCY: Oh, no—

REVEREND TODD: Will you join us for dinner?

NANCY: No, I couldn't—

BUD: I won't embarrass you.

NANCY: No, I think.

BUD: I insist.

NANCY: Please—

REVEREND TODD: Please join us.

NANCY: I don't think I should.

REVEREND TODD: Nancy? You promised?

## SCENE 10

[*Sound: a ringing telephone.* KEN *answers a telephone. Isolated elsewhere, on the phone,* ASHLEY.]

KEN: Hello?

ASHLEY: Hello, Daddy, it's me, Ashley.

KEN: Hi.

ASHLEY: What are you doing?

KEN: Hi, sweetheart, um . . . I'm just. I just got out of the shower, and I'm about to walk and get a sandwich somewhere.

ASHLEY: Mm. How's London?

KEN: It's great. Today is really extraordinary. It's a little cold and windy, but the air is really clear and bright.

ASHLEY: Sounds lovely.

KEN: It is, it truly is.

ASHLEY: I don't mean to spoil your beautiful day, but I thought you should know your wife isn't doing so hot. She's very depressed and she's having a problem with weeping, with uncontrollable weeping. She can't drive, she can't go to the store—

KEN: Because of her weeping problem—

ASHLEY: Yeah, I finally convinced her to get some antidepressants from Dr. Block, but I don't think she's taking them.

KEN: That's. I don't know what to say. I am sorry.

ASHLEY: So you're sorry? Great. That's the only reason I called. Bye.

KEN: Ashley?

ASHLEY: You know, no, I'm not hanging up. I think you need to hear what I think of you.

KEN: All right.

[*Silence.*]

ASHLEY: Are you planning on coming home? Any time soon?

KEN: No time soon.

ASHLEY: Are you planning on coming home?

KEN: No time soon.

ASHLEY: At all?

KEN: Yes.

ASHLEY: When?

KEN: I don't know.

ASHLEY: What are you doing there?

KEN: Well, I'm sculpting.

ASHLEY: You're what?

KEN: I'm sculpting. I'm learning sculpture, the art of sculpture. I've made a couple of good friends here, whom I care about, and they inspire me, and one of them is a very gifted sculptor, and he's teaching me, being very patient with me, and I'm enjoying myself. That's what I'm doing. You asked me, and that's what I'm doing.

ASHLEY: And God? Wasn't there something about God?

KEN: I'm—

ASHLEY: I mean, wasn't that the reason for all this? Weren't you feeling very confused—

KEN: I—

ASHLEY: —by your feelings about God, your doubts? Your faith, your belief—

KEN: Yes—

ASHLEY: —was challenged, or questioned, and so that's why you felt the need to abandon your family—?

KEN: You're not letting me talk—

ASHLEY: You've been gone now six weeks?

KEN: Do you want to hear what I have to say or not?

ASHLEY: Maybe not.

KEN: All right.

ASHLEY: Yes. I want to hear what you have to say.

KEN: This is all very complicated and confusing for me. But when I'm working away on my silly little sculpture, I feel less confused—

ASHLEY: All right. Great. That's great. Good luck with your sculpture career.

KEN: Does your mother know you're calling me?

ASHLEY: Are you kidding? She'd kill me.

KEN: How's everybody else? How are Greg and the kids?

ASHLEY: As far as I'm concerned, you've forfeited the right to ask those questions.

# SCENE 11

[*Sound: Ellington's "Fleurette Africaine."* TAMYRA *and* HARRY's *flat.* TAMYRA *poses for* HARRY *and* KEN. *She wears only a thin piece of fabric draped over her lap. She is in the same pose as* HARRY's *half-finished sculpture: head tilted back, arms raised to the heavens.* KEN's *sculpture depicts a life-size head and neck, made of blue-gray clay. Compared to* HARRY's *work,* KEN's *statue is crude, amateur, almost childlike.* HARRY *works on his sculpture in an involved, meticulous fashion. He backs away, lights a smoke, studies his work. Now he notices* KEN *struggling, and, gently,* HARRY *approaches.*]

HARRY: Sometimes it helps to exaggerate just a bit.

KEN: How do you mean?

HARRY: You're not hoping to actually recreate Tamyra, you're hoping to *interpret* her. Yes? Translate her. Through your language.

KEN: Okay . . .

[HARRY *crosses to* TAMYRA, *traces his forefinger along her neck.*]

HARRY: You see? The line of her neck?

KEN: The line.

HARRY: Like you drew it before, with the charcoals?

KEN: Yes.

HARRY: Her head is tilted . . . ?

KEN: Right.

HARRY: Maybe just exaggerate that. Just a bit.

KEN: Tilt the head more?

HARRY: Yes.

KEN: I'm sorry, why again?

HARRY: *Or* tilt it less. But tilt it *more.*

KEN: Because that's, I'm *translating* her.

HARRY: There's no point in producing Tamyra *again:* she already exists. I mean, yes, you want to have the *ability* to do that: that's *craft.* But your belief, your expression of your belief: that's *art.*

KEN: All right.

HARRY: It's simplistic, but: objectivity is craft, subjectivity is art.

KEN: Right. So tilt the head back.

HARRY: Yes.

[KEN *bends back the head on his sculpture and it breaks off in his hand.*]

KEN: Fudge.

HARRY: Goddamn it, use a little fucking sensitivity! You're not bricking up a hole in the wall! Try a softer touch!

KEN: I'm sorry—

HARRY: You're like some ape, one of those fucking apes from *2001,* bashing bones together—!

KEN: I'm just not accustomed—

HARRY: Useless shite!

[HARRY *storms out.* KEN *hands* TAMYRA *a robe. She lights up.*]

TAMYRA: He's actually much more patient than I would have expected.

KEN: I wish I was better.

TAMYRA: You just started. You know how long he's been doing this?

KEN: I don't have to become great at it.

TAMYRA: No, but you want to get better. As it should be.

KEN: Do you think I'm wasting my time?

TAMYRA: Do you think you're wasting your time?

KEN: No.

TAMYRA: I think you're wasting your money.

KEN: Because I'm *hopeless*.

TAMYRA: Because you've been so generous with both of us. You could've got lessons for a lot less than our rent payment.

KEN: You're my friends.

TAMYRA: Yes. We are. You remember what I said to you that day back at the Sheraton? That the reason I was nice to you was because of your money.

KEN: Yes.

TAMYRA: That isn't true. I'm actually quite fond of you. And I think in your own way, you're very brave.

KEN: Now I'm embarrassed.

TAMYRA: Then you embarrass easily . . .

KEN: "The sky folds its wings over you,
Lifting you, carrying you to my arms
With its punctual, mysterious courtesy.

That's why I sing to the day and to the moon,
To the sea, to time, and all the planets,
To your daily voice, to your nocturnal skin."

TAMYRA: What is that?

KEN: Pablo Neruda.

[KEN *and* TAMYRA *stand close. A moment lingers. She smiles warmly at him, but there's another look: this is not going any further. She takes the sculpted clay head from his hand, crosses to his sculpture.*]

TAMYRA: This isn't me at all, is it? This is you. Self-portrait. Tell me, who will you show this to?

KEN: Do I have to show it to anybody?

TAMYRA: None of this means anything without a witness.

[*She gently works at affixing the head to the statue.*]

This isn't bad . . .


## SEVENTH MOVEMENT, PART 1

### SCENE 12

[*Sound: television.* KEN *and* NANCY's *living room.* NANCY *and* BUD *watch TV:* Touched by an Angel, *say. They watch. They watch. The program ends.*]

BUD: They oughta make more shows like that one, you know it?

NANCY: Mm-hm.

BUD: Just good stories. About good people. I swear, some of these other programs, the language they use . . .

NANCY: Mm-hm.

BUD: Make me think I'm back in the Army.

NANCY: Can I get you something else, Bud?

BUD: Dear, I believe I've had a God's plenty and an ample sufficiency.

NANCY: I have some peach cobbler.

BUD: Did you bake me a peach pie?

NANCY: It's from the Winn-Dixie.

BUD: No, thank you.

[*Silence.*]

What's coming on now?

[NANCY *yawns.*]

Hm?

NANCY: What?

BUD: What's coming on now?

NANCY: I don't know. It's getting to be my bath time.

BUD: Is it.

NANCY: Yes, it is.

[BUD *clicks the remote, kills the TV. They sit.*]

BUD: Say, I sure like being with you, Nanny Goat. Anyone ever call you that? Nanny Goat?

NANCY: No.

BUD: Mind if I do?

NANCY: Oh.

[*They sit.*]

BUD: You know. I've buried so many of my friends, I got calluses on my hands from carrying caskets. Folks my age, or who would be my age. It's tough, sometimes, just to find people you can sit with, talk to.

NANCY: You seem to do all right.

BUD: I mean folks you *want* to spend time with, who still have some spark left in them. Like you for me. And I hope . . . me for you.

[*She smiles.*]

[*Sings tunelessly*] "And you . . . for me, and tea for two . . ."

[*He leans in for a kiss. NANCY does not respond; in fact, she keeps her gaze fixed on the dark television.*]

Nanny Goat . . .

NANCY: Hm?

BUD: You see me here?

NANCY: Mm-hm.

BUD: Won't you kiss me, dear heart?

NANCY: I want you to stop it, please. I'm very uncomfortable.

BUD: I just like being with you. I just want to be close.

NANCY: I'm married.

BUD: Just a kiss.

NANCY: No.

BUD: Just one kiss.

NANCY: No.

BUD: You want me to chase you?

NANCY: That talk is out of line. I'm married. Please behave like a gentleman.

BUD: You don't appear very married to me.

NANCY: How things appear to you isn't my concern. I am a happily married woman.

BUD: That's why you've been keeping company with me every night?

NANCY: I haven't invited you; you've invited yourself.

BUD: So you don't want me here.

NANCY: Not if you're going to behave like this. Ken is taking some time for himself, and I am respecting his wish to do so. In the meanwhile, I've been lonely and . . . and I've enjoyed your company.

BUD: Your husband has left you.

NANCY: He did not leave me. We're taking some time apart.

BUD: Yeah, I took some time away from Ginny's mom. Round about forty years.

NANCY: Ken is coming home.

[BUD *stands, grabs his hat and coat.*]

BUD: I'm seventy-five years old. I know some things. Not a lot, but some. It's a man's nature to strike out into the world, endeavor, explore. Ken was a fine husband and father for a good long while, but that's over now. He is in the World. But I am done with that part of my life, ready to ride out my remaining time. In comfort. And, if you'll have me, with company.

NANCY: Good night, Bud.

BUD: So you wait for him: good. You'll give that up eventually. And then maybe you and me'll have some things to talk about.

[*He starts to exit, stops.*]

You just have to ask yourself: Why would he come back?

[*He leaves.*]

## SCENE 13

[*Sound: television, oxygen inhaler.* CAMMIE's *private room.* CAMMIE *sits in her wheelchair, pointed toward a TV game show:* Wheel of Fortune, *say. The volume is quite loud.* CAMMIE's *oxygen mask is off. She sits. She sits. She breathes.* NANCY *sits beside her. They sit. They watch television. They sit.* CAMMIE *coughs.* NANCY *turns, studies her.* CAMMIE's *coughing is deep, strained. Her breaths become long and labored.* NANCY *stares at her.* CAMMIE *struggles for air.* NANCY *stares at her.* NANCY *stares at her.*]

## SCENE 14

[KEN's *hotel room.* KEN *sleeps in the darkened room. He wakes, sits up, aware of another presence in the room: a figure, sitting alone, obscured by shadow.*]

KEN: Mom . . . ?!

[*Beat.*]

What are you doing here?

[*Beat.*]

I'm sorry.

[*Beat.*]

I'm sorry for that place. That you were in that place.

[*Beat.*]

I prayed for you to go. I prayed for him to take you. I prayed for it to end. I prayed for you to die. I prayed for you to die. I prayed for you to die.

[*The phone rings. The phone rings. The phone rings.*]

# SEVENTH MOVEMENT, PART 2

## SCENE 15

[*Sound: knocking.* TAMYRA *and* HARRY's *flat.* HARRY, *bleary eyed, wearing a tattered robe, shuffles to the door.*]

HARRY: Who the fuck's there?

KEN [*from offstage*]: It's me. It's Ken.

[HARRY *opens the door.* KEN *enters, wet, disheveled.*]

HARRY: It's five in the morning.

KEN: I know.

HARRY: I must've been asleep for an hour.

KEN: Is Tamyra here?

HARRY: No, she's gone to Brighton for the weekend. With a friend.

KEN: Oh, God.

HARRY: Anything I can help you with?

KEN: I just needed to see her.

HARRY: She's in Brighton.

KEN: I just . . .

HARRY: It's five in the morning. You look awful.

KEN: I got some bad news.

HARRY: This calls for hashish.

[HARRY *scouts for a hash pipe.*]

KEN: What? No.

HARRY: Well, maybe not for you. You might want a fried egg. Me, I'm going the hashish route. So what's the problem today?

KEN: I've been walking.

HARRY: That's nice.

KEN: I walked here.

HARRY: Right. From the West End?

KEN: My daughter called me.

HARRY: Don't tell me that bitch took my hash pipe to Brighton.

KEN: My mother died.

[HARRY *stops.*]

My mom . . .

[HARRY crosses to KEN, puts an arm around his shoulder.]

I didn't know where to go.

HARRY: It's okay.

KEN: I didn't have anywhere to go.

HARRY: You came here.

KEN: Where am I.

HARRY: You're here.

KEN: You're a stranger.

HARRY: Yeah.

KEN: Thank you.

HARRY: Let's work.

KEN: Now.

HARRY: Absolutely.

[HARRY crosses to his sculpture, turns on the boom box. Monk's solo
"'Round Midnight." HARRY works. KEN studies HARRY, then approaches
his own sculpture. He stares at the bust, uncomprehending. He grips the
edges of his worktable, bows his head. Then he digs his hands into the
clay, destroying the sculpture. He becomes engrossed in the work,
changing the work, working the clay, kneading the clay. He sculpts a
crude shape from the clay. He stops, takes in his new creation, looks up,
out. He quickly grabs his coat, goes to the door. Stops, turns, looks
to HARRY. They share a look. HARRY almost imperceptibly nods. KEN
leaves.]

# SCENE 16

[*Sound: organ music. A funeral home. A rectangle of light representing a casket.* ASHLEY *stands, studying* CAMMIE. KEN *enters, crosses to her. She looks up, sees him. They hug, then turn their attention back to* CAMMIE.]

ASHLEY: She looks peaceful.

KEN: Does she?

ASHLEY: Don't you think?

KEN: Where's your mother?

ASHLEY: She's around here somewhere.

[*Beat.*]

Natalie's not coming in.

KEN: That's okay.

ASHLEY: Is it.

KEN: It's not okay with you.

ASHLEY: No, it's not.

KEN: You're awful hard on people, Ashley.

ASHLEY: You're going to lecture me?

KEN: Did that sound like a lecture?

ASHLEY: I know what it was.

[*Silence.* NANCY *enters, unseen by* KEN *and* ASHLEY.]

What happened to you? I don't know you at all.

KEN: That's my fault. We can change that.

ASHLEY: Greg thinks you're going to hell.

KEN: Greg's a fool.

ASHLEY: I think he's right.

KEN: Then you're a fool, too.

[ASHLEY *exits, passing* NANCY. KEN *and* NANCY *cross to each other, hug. They stand beside each other and look into the casket.*]

## SCENE 17

[*Sound: suburban street sounds. A luxury sedan.* KEN *and* NANCY *sit in the parked car.*]

NANCY: Since you left, all I've wanted is to have you home. Now you're here . . .

KEN: You want me to leave.

[*She nods.*]

NANCY: I don't trust you, Ken.

KEN: I would have done things differently . . . if I had been able. Nancy, I am sorry I hurt you.

NANCY: I understand you well enough to know you aren't a malicious person.

[*Silence.*]

Do you believe in God?

KEN: I think so.

NANCY: You feel better.

KEN: Yes.

NANCY: Good. I'm glad. I am glad you're feeling better.

KEN: Nancy . . .

NANCY: Will you go back to London?

KEN: I didn't come back here for Mom. I came here for you.

[*Beat.*]

I don't know where I want to go or what I want to do. But I want you with me. I want us to be together.

[*Silence.* NANCY *stares ahead.*]

Did you hear what I said?

NANCY: Yes.

[KEN *tries to touch* NANCY, *but she pulls away.*]

You tore it up.

[*He tries again. She pulls away again.*]

You . . .

[*He takes her arm and she attacks him, raining slaps and punches onto his body, growling and grunting from the exertion. He does not protect himself.*]

## GODDAMN YOU . . . GODDAMN YOU!

*[She collapses, weeping.]*

You tore it up . . .

KEN: Nancy . . .

NANCY: Now it's nothing . . .

KEN: Come with me.

NANCY: It's nothing . . .

KEN: I need you.

NANCY: . . . nothing . . . just pieces . . .

KEN: Please.

NANCY: . . . just . . .

KEN: Just you and me.

NANCY: . . . just scraps . . .

KEN: I want you to come with me.

NANCY: . . . ashes . . .

KEN: I need you to come with me.

NANCY: How do I do that?

KEN: You do it.

NANCY: I don't know how.

KEN: We'll start something new.

NANCY: You want to start something new.

KEN: Yes.

NANCY: With me.

KEN: I love you, and I want us to start something new.

NANCY: You love me.

KEN: Come with me.

NANCY: You want me.

KEN: Yes.

NANCY: Really.

KEN: We're partners.

NANCY: We are.

KEN: Yes.

NANCY: I'm your partner.

KEN: You've always been my partner.

NANCY: I don't feel that.

KEN: I know. I'm sorry.

[*He slowly extends his hand to her, palm upward. She studies it.*]

I choose you. Choose me.

[*She studies him. She tentatively takes his hand. They look at each other, then turn and look ahead. Stars appear above them.*]

MICHAEL BROSILOW

Nancy (Rondi Reed) and Ken Carpenter (Rick Snyder)
sing, "Master, I hear thy call" at their Baptist church.

Nancy (Rondi Reed) and Ken Carpenter (Rick Snyder) perform their nightly routine; Nancy rubs on hand lotion, and Ken prays.

MICHAEL BROSILOW

Ken (Rick Snyder) collapses in the bathroom, staggered to find he no longer believes in God.

MICHAEL BROSILOW

Ken (Rick Snyder) and Nancy Carpenter (Rondi Reed) contemplate how to handle Ken's lack of faith at the beginning of the second movement.

MICHAEL BROSILOW

Ken Carpenter (Rick Snyder) and fellow passenger Pat Monday (Shannon Cochran) meet in flight to London.

Ken Carpenter (Rick Snyder) discusses the artistic process with sculptor
Harry Brown (Michael Shannon), as Tamyra (Karen Aldridge) models.

MICHAEL BROSILOW

Harry Brown (Michael Shannon) and Ken Carpenter (Rick Snyder)

Nancy (Rondi Reed) and Ken Carpenter (Rick Snyder) settle scores at the end of the play.

# ABOUT THE PLAYWRIGHT

An ensemble member of the Steppenwolf Theatre Company, Tracy Letts is an actor, a director, and a playwright who, in addition to his stage credits, has appeared in several motion pictures and television shows.